2/,0

More than **four** million children and up to **4** percent of adults in the United States live with some form of ADHD.

Photographs © 2007: Alamy Images/Scott Camazine: 51; Art
Directors and TRIP Photo Library/Helene Rogers: 39; Corbis Images: 55
(Lester V. Bergman), 117 (Bettmann), 34 (Laura Dwight), 86 (Ole Graf), 25
(Charles Gupton), 12 (Gabe Palmer), 23 (Michelle Pedone/zefa), 77
(Jose Luis Pelaez, Inc.), 19 (Jose Luis Pelaez/zefa), 89 (Brent C. Petersen),
91 (Ariel Skelley), 101 (Lacassagne Xavier/Sygma); Getty Images: 107
(Bruce Ayres/Stone), 119 (Tim Clary/AFP), 53 (CMSP/Science Faction),
42 (Christina Kennedy/DK Stock), 31 (Michael Malyszko/Taxi), 111
(Nancy Ney/Digital Vision), 108 (SW Productions/Photodisc Green);
Index Stock Imagery: 99 (Menachem Mandell), 83 (Network Productions);
JupiterImages/Rubberball: 40; Monty Stilson: cover; Omni-Photo
Communications/Laura Dwight: 37; Photo Researchers, NY: 32 (Ken Lax),
49 (David M. Phillips); PhotoEdit: 80 (Mary Kate Denny), 70 (Michael
Newman), 8, 43 (David Young-Wolff); Richard Hutchings Photography: 17;
The Image Works/Bob Daemmrich: 15; Visuals Unlimited/Science VU: 63.

Cover design by The Design Lab
Book design by The Design Lab

Library of Congress Cataloging-in-Publication Data
Petersen, Christine.
  Does everyone have ADHD? : a teen's guide to diagnosis and
treatment / by Christine Petersen.
    p. cm.
  Includes bibliographical references and index.
  ISBN-10: 0-531-16794-1 (lib. bdg.)   0-531-17975-3 (pbk.)
  ISBN-13: 978-0-531-16794-6 (lib. bdg.)   978-0-531-17975-8 (pbk.)
   1. Attention-deficit-disordered children—Juvenile literature
  2. Hyperactive children—Behavior modification—Juvenile literature.
  3. Senses and sensation in children—Juvenile literature. I. Title.
   RJ506.H9P48 2006
   618.92'8589—dc22   2005024625

Does everyone have ADHD?

A Teen's Guide to Diagnosis and Treatment

by Christine Petersen

Franklin Watts®

A Division of Scholastic Inc.
New York • Toronto • London • Auckland • Sydney
Mexico City • New Delhi • Hong Kong
Danbury, Connecticut

[contents]

part two
Living Well with ADHD

Part one:
Understanding ADHD

chapter 1
What Is ADHD?

It's a cold December day outside a suburban middle school. Inside, a group of seventh graders listen distractedly as their teacher finishes a lesson, their attention diverted by the sight of snow falling outside the window. This is the year's first good snowfall, and they are eager to be out in it.

Disregarding the teacher's reminders to finish his worksheet, twelve-year-old James leaps out of his chair and runs to the window. "Snow, snow, snow!" he chants while drumming his hands on the windowsill in time with the words. He turns to the teacher, his eyes gleaming. "Can we go out yet?"

Some people with ADHD have a difficult time staying focused at school.

"Finish your work, James. The period ends in ten minutes," is the response. "You can sit by the window if you want, but I need your paper—and your homework—when the bell rings."

Across the room, James's classmate Casey sits quietly in her seat, head resting on her folded arms atop the desk. She too is gazing toward the snow-covered schoolyard, but she seems more mesmerized than energized. On her desk is a half-finished worksheet.

When the bell rings, James scoops up his books and papers. Forgetting to turn in both the worksheet and the homework, he is out the door like a shot. After tossing everything into his locker, he scans the surroundings. His eyes fall onto a piece of rolled-up poster board leaning against the wall. A broad grin spreads across his face, and he grabs the roll and sprints for the door. He moves so fast that his coat is still half off as he runs toward the hill above the parking lot.

The rest of the students file out of the classroom, chatting as they head for their lockers or outside with friends. The last to leave the room, Casey stops at the teacher's desk to drop off her incomplete worksheet, then ambles out the door. She steps outside alone and walks in the general direction of her classmates, stopping to sit at the bottom of the hill.

James, meanwhile, has climbed the hill and unrolled the poster board. Catching sight of Casey below him, he hollers, "Hey! Come up for a ride! We'll go faster with two of us to add weight!"

Casey shakes her head. "You're on your own," she says.

Rolling his eyes, James lays the poster board on the ground and plops himself atop it. "You're such a loser!" he taunts. Giving himself a hard shove, he sets the "sled" in motion. It slips rapidly down the snow-covered bank. Then, halfway to the bottom, it hits a hidden rock and jumps sideways. Laughing despite the jolt, James throws himself onto his side and rolls the rest of the way down the hill, narrowly missing a parked car as he hits the pavement.

More than four million children and up to 4 percent of adults in the United States live with some form of ADHD.

"Who's the loser now?" mutters Casey.

Although their behaviors are radically different, James and Casey both have attention-deficit/hyperactivity disorder (ADHD). ADHD is a health and mental **disorder** that affects learning, behavior, and perception.

ADHD usually shows up in elementary- or middle school–aged children. Symptoms include **hyperactivity** (moving too fast), **impulsivity** (acting before thinking), or **inattention** (inability to concentrate or pay attention).[1] Along with these symptoms, young people with ADHD may have difficulty sleeping, show signs of anger or depression, be very disorganized, and have learning disabilities. Together, these symptoms make children with ADHD seem less mature than their peers.

The respected Greek philosopher and healer Hippocrates wrote about ADHD-type behaviors more than 2,400 years ago. He had no idea why the behaviors occurred, and for centuries, no one else did either.[2]

[ADHD in History]

It might seem as if ADHD is a product of our modern world, especially because the disorder has gotten so much attention lately in the media. In fact, an awareness of ADHD-type behaviors actually dates far back into human history. Prior to the twentieth century, poor parenting was often blamed for the symptoms. When kids failed at school, teachers were held responsible. And very often, kids with ADHD were accused of being naughty or lazy.

A DIFFERENT VIEWPOINT

This perception began to change in the twentieth century. In 1902, British pediatrician Sir George Frederic Still was working with a group of boys and girls who exhibited severe levels of hyperactivity, aggression, impulsivity, and a tendency toward emotional outbursts. Dr. Still took an innovative viewpoint toward these behaviors: he believed that they resulted from physical changes in the brain.

Besides observing the children, Dr. Still collected information about their families, which revealed two important facts. First, many of the children came from "stable" (healthy) homes. And second, many of the children's parents or other family members also had mental health problems, including alcoholism and depression.[3] Dr. Still wrote up his findings and presented them to other physicians at the Royal College of Medicine. He concluded that kids were hyperactive or inattentive either because they had received a damaging brain injury or because they had inherited those tendencies from their parents. Either way, he said that kids and parents shouldn't be called "bad" because of it.

Behaviors such as not listening to instructions before beginning assignments can lead to poor grades for students with ADHD.

ADHD is actually a term that covers several related disorders. The one thing that people with ADHD seem to have in common is a reduced ability to filter out sights, sounds, and activities that are not related to what they are supposed to be doing.

Symptoms of ADHD cause day-to-day problems with learning, behavior, and the ability to make and maintain relationships. For example, a child with ADHD may begin working on an assignment before getting all the instructions. People with ADHD sometimes find it hard to follow rules of politeness. They shout out answers in class rather than waiting to be called on, interrupt during conversations, or act unruly in ways that frustrate others.

Along with all other known neurological and mental disorders (those occurring in the brain and mind), ADHD is described in the book *Diagnostic and Statistical Manual of Mental Disorders, Fourth Edition* (DSM-IV-TR). This massive volume is published by the American Psychiatric Association and updated every few years. (The DSM-IV-TR was updated in 2000.) It contains details on the behaviors and symptoms used to diagnose a disorder.

Psychologists or physicians usually organize the **assessment** process for ADHD. They observe the child in as many settings as possible (for example, when playing as well as when doing homework). Various medical and psychological tests are given to the child. The results are compared to questionnaires completed by parents, teachers, and other adults involved in the child's life. All are then compared to the DSM.

ADHD can make it difficult for people to learn and then apply what they learn in new situations.

[White Noise]

Imagine this. You're sitting in the living room, trying to read a chapter of homework. At the same time, one of your siblings is watching TV and munching on popcorn. Another is typing on the computer. Down the hall, your mother is talking and laughing on the phone. Outside, birds are singing and a lawn mower is humming in the distance. This is a tremendous amount of activity! Amazingly, most people's brains are able to take in this much **stimuli** (occurrences that catch a person's attention) at once—including sights, sounds, tastes, touches, smells, and activities—and filter out what is not important. This is how we are able to concentrate.

If you don't have ADHD, this situation might be a little distracting. But chances are, once you focused your attention on the reading, most of the sounds would gradually fade away from your awareness. But a person with ADHD would find it difficult, or perhaps even impossible, to tune out this multitude of sounds. Everything would be heard clearly with no filters and no fading. As a result, it would be impossible to concentrate on the reading. And sadly, without the ability to focus, very little learning can take place.

The DSM defines three major categories of ADHD (although there may eventually turn out to be many more): hyperactive/impulsive-type, inattentive-type, and combined-type. In general, an individual must exhibit a minimum of six of the symptoms in a particular category to be diagnosed with ADHD. At least a few of the symptoms need to have shown up before the age of seven. Symptoms must also have a negative impact on the person's ability to function in at least two settings, for example at school and at home.[4]

When younger children are being assessed for ADHD, doctors look for evidence that the symptoms have continued for six months or more.

Doctors must do a thorough evaluation of a patient before making a diagnosis of ADHD.

Hyperactive/Impulsive-Type ADHD

Because hyperactivity and impulsiveness stand out so clearly, they were the first symptoms to alert physicians more than a hundred years ago that attention disorders existed.

Hyperactivity can be tricky to diagnose because the symptoms tend to vary, depending on the situation. For example, when engaged in calm tasks or normal play, a hyperactive boy may behave much like other children—he may play quietly and show no signs of the disorder. If the situation becomes too complex or stressful, however, he is likely to begin talking very loudly and moving quickly around the room.

Impulsiveness reveals itself in overstimulating environments as well. Mild sources of stress cause children with this type of ADHD to become intensely emotional. The stress may prompt a temper tantrum or crying; the child may speak rudely or lash out physically. Although they may be familiar with rules and want to follow them, hyperactive/impulsive

Although boys and girls can have any form of ADHD, boys appear more likely to exhibit the hyperactive/impulsive type.

Some people with ADHD have a hard time controlling their impulses. As a result, they may hit other people or break things when they are angry or frustrated.

Hyperactive children may hit objects or other people, or they might engage in silly or outrageous behavior.

children may be unable to use their mental "brakes" to stop a behavior.

Girls with hyperactive/impulsive-type ADHD tend to show slightly different symptoms than boys. They may tend to be a bit tomboyish, gravitating toward boys as friends. In no way do all girls who enjoy sports have ADHD, but girls with the disorder may find that the activity and social aspects of team sports suit their personalities well. These girls may be inclined to participate in the kinds of risky behaviors that are usually associated with boys. Hyperactive/impulsive-type ADHD can also show itself in girls through excessive socializing and talking.

17

Inattentive-Type ADHD

Inattention and distractibility are characteristic of this type of ADHD, which was not recognized until late in the twentieth century. It appears to be more common among girls than boys. Unfortunately, "dreamy" behavior is considered normal in adolescent girls, as is a tendency to be less assertive. Thus, girls with inattentive-type ADHD can be overlooked. Boys with this form of ADHD may stand out a little more, as this behavior is more unusual for them—or these boys may just be perceived as unmotivated, lazy, or poor students. As a result, as little as 30 percent of children who have this type of ADHD may be diagnosed.

It may seem as though people with inattentive-type ADHD are not paying attention to anything.

"ADHD is the most common psychiatric condition affecting children, estimates of prevalence in childhood range from five to ten percent."

—National Mental Health Association[5]

Inattentive-type ADHD reveals itself most clearly in three settings: those that are overstimulating, those that are boring, and those that involve many new stimuli.

Cell phones and other devices can be particularly distracting for students with ADHD.

In reality, they are aware of everything because their brains are unable to filter out the less-important pieces of information to focus on a single important part.

When subjected to too much information at once, inattentive-type ADHD sufferers may appear to "zone out"—they retreat from the stimuli in order to protect themselves from it. Or they may focus the most attention on any stimulus that is new. In either case, returning one's attention to the task at hand can be extremely difficult.

Repetitive, understimulating situations (especially those that don't allow for any form of activity or movement) can also lead to total inattention. When bored, these kids may divert all their attention to a completely different stimulus: they may stare out the window at leaves fluttering in the breeze, for example, or become wrapped up in spinning a pencil on their desk.

Combined-Type ADHD

Some people exhibit symptoms from both categories. To be diagnosed with this type of ADHD, at least six symptoms of hyperactivity/impulsivity, along with at least six of inattention, must be identified (see sidebar).

[Behaviors Associated with ADHD]

The DSM lists many criteria for diagnosing the various types of ADHD. The following is a modified list, giving a general idea of the symptoms and behaviors associated with ADHD.

A HYPERACTIVE/IMPULSIVE PERSON

- is "on the go" almost constantly, as if unable to control his or her movements
- fidgets or squirms when required to sit for long periods of time, or feels restless in such situations
- becomes frustrated or sleepy when forced to be still
- is unable to do the same task for long; moves from one activity to another
- talks rapidly and frequently
- blurts out thoughts or interrupts when other people are talking
- has trouble waiting for a turn to speak or participate in an activity
- takes risks that others would avoid

AN INATTENTIVE PERSON

- usually has trouble focusing attention on a single activity for more than a few minutes at a time
- may sometimes hyperfocus (become completely engaged in an activity and unaware of other things happening nearby) when involved in a task that is really interesting
- may be easily distracted by activities or sounds

(continued on next page)

- finds it difficult to sort through the many stimuli in the surrounding environment and may "zone out" when experiencing overstimulation
- has trouble listening
- has a hard time following instructions or paying attention to details
- often starts tasks but does not complete them

Although you may feel isolated if you experience any of these symptoms, remember that as many as 7 percent of Americans under the age of eighteen have ADHD[6]—so chances are, you already know someone who has it. If you receive this diagnosis, there are teachers and other professionals who can help you work around (and with) your symptoms, allowing you to learn and succeed.

ADHD commonly affects what are called "executive functions": the ability to organize and plan, to reason and keep emotions under control, to transition smoothly between tasks, and to utilize short-term memory (meaning the ability to recall very recent events or to repeat information that was just learned).

Keeping emotions under control is often difficult for people who struggle with ADHD.

Other Symptoms of ADHD

Several other behaviors seem to be shared by many people with ADHD, regardless of which formal category they fit into. These include clumsiness or poor physical coordination, difficulty with social relationships, a need for instant gratification, and a tendency to seek out stimulating experiences.

Disorganization makes it hard for people with ADHD to keep track of belongings such as keys and schoolwork. It also affects their ability to be on time. The term *disorganized* can be used to describe the physical abilities of some people with ADHD. In some people, ADHD causes the kind of visual problems that can be corrected by eyeglasses. In others, the brain cannot effectively interpret what the eyes see. Whichever is the case, poor vision is sure to contribute to problems with everyday coordination.

As many as 40 percent of adolescents with ADHD are arrested before the age of 21. That's twice the rate of kids who don't have ADHD.[7]

While some kids with ADHD are highly social and have no trouble making friends, others find friendship to be a challenge. Adolescence is a time when most young people want to fit in. But kids with ADHD often can't control their behavior. Their own tendency to be aggressive, and therefore to seem bossy (or even dangerous), isolates them from peers.

Such rejection may make them pull away from other people. It can also lead them to spend time with other "different" kids, who may reinforce their tendency to get into trouble. Extremely isolated kids with ADHD can begin to act out against society by taking part in criminal activity.

ADHD Later in Life

ADHD is a lifelong disorder. But there's good news for many people who experience it. With maturity, significant changes in symptoms often occur—especially if the individual has set up a beneficial treatment plan and maintained it over the years. Some degree of **remission** (a lessening or disappearance of symptoms) often occurs in adulthood, as well. Hyperactivity tends to shift to a general sense of restlessness in young adults. Impulsiveness usually declines as teenagers gain life experience and build coping skills. Inattention may be the most common symptom among adults.

Unfortunately, adults with untreated (or poorly managed) ADHD are at significant risk of becoming involved in criminal activity. They are also more likely to use drugs, alcohol, and cigarettes to relieve symptoms or to help them forget about social problems.

Some people with ADHD have the urge to pursue stimulating experiences. This is called **sensation-seeking behavior**. It's the brain's way of trying to force itself into action when the person feels disengaged or uninterested in the activity at hand. Sensation-seeking behavior may be harmless, such as when a child sits for long periods of time playing a fast-paced computer game. However, it may also lead people to try dangerous activities such as driving very fast or doing high-risk sports. This is related to the desire for instant gratification that so often accompanies ADHD.

Substance abuse is another form of sensation seeking. Some people with ADHD develop dangerous habits, such as drug or alcohol abuse, in an attempt to relieve symptoms or experience new sensations. Other habits may seem less dangerous, but they can still cause difficulties in day-to-day living. The frequent use of coffee, caffeinated sodas, or other high-caffeine drinks temporarily improves symptoms, but those symptoms often become worse when the **stimulant** wears off. Stimulant pills to prevent sleepiness can cause similar problems, as well as potentially causing weight loss or long-term heart problems.

Smoking, too, produces a confusing chemical reaction in the brain. In particular, the nicotine in tobacco stimulates chemicals that seem to relieve some ADHD symptoms. Unfortunately, nicotine is a strongly addictive substance. Kids with ADHD are more susceptible to all these abuses than their peers.[8]

chapter 2

Diagnosing ADHD

All of the symptoms of ADHD are normal human behaviors. Almost everyone has had moments of distraction or hyperactivity, been disorganized, or acted impulsively. The important distinction is that, for most people, these are short-term problems that result from illness, lack of sleep, intake of stimulants (such as caffeine), or stress. In these cases, the symptoms usually occur in only one setting. For example, a student might show inattention in French class because that class is held first thing in the morning when he or she is sleepy, but the same student is attentive in other subjects and at home.

As most parents of teens know, the usual "growing pains" of adolescence can also make kids behave in ways that seem similar to ADHD. Teens sometimes ignore instructions, fail to follow through on tasks, or are hostile. They may be frustrated with themselves, have social conflicts, and be distracted at school. The critical word in the previous description is *sometimes*. People with ADHD exhibit some of these behaviors every day and in at least two settings, and they are usually unable to control them without therapy or other treatment.

Even if an observer isn't familiar with ADHD, a child with frequent hyperactivity, inattention, or impulsivity stands out. Unfortunately, children with ADHD are often labeled as difficult or lazy long before someone suggests that they be evaluated. This happens because symptoms can vary greatly from one day to the next, depending on the child's overall health and how much pressure the child is under. On some days, symptoms are extremely evident, while

Diagnosis of ADHD typically begins when someone notices that a child is experiencing one or more of the major ADHD symptoms.

Quantitative tests often use materials from the body, such as blood or urine, to look for evidence of a specific illness or disorder. Other types of quantitative tests, such as X-rays, can provide an image of the affected area of the body.

on others they may almost seem to disappear. To untrained observers, it can look as if the child just isn't trying or chooses to misbehave.

The other difficulty in diagnosing ADHD is that there is no single, simple test that can confirm its presence. Many health problems can be identified using what medical professionals call quantitative tests—tests that provide measurable results. In most cases, an ADHD diagnosis is made by comparing information about the child's learning and behavior to the DSM criteria.

While an increasing number of ADHD cases are being recognized in preschool, most go unnoticed or undiagnosed until children enter into the formal school system. In this setting, symptoms seem to become more severe because kids are suddenly expected to keep track of books and materials, sit quietly for long stretches of time, behave nicely, and manage homework. Sometimes an older child is having trouble learning or getting along with others, realizes it, and brings it up to an adult. More often, however, children don't realize that anything is wrong—after all, they have no other experience to provide a comparison. Usually a teacher, parent, coach, or other adult notices the symptoms and calls attention to them. The next step is to visit a doctor.

In order to gain a complete picture of a child's physical and mental health, as well as his or her behavior and abilities at home and at school, many people must work together. Medical doctors and psychologists, parents, teachers, and the child each contribute pieces to the puzzle of an ADHD assessment.[1]

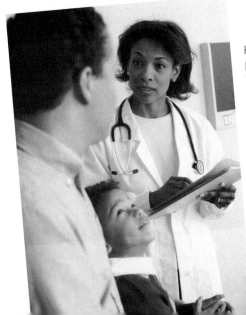

Health care professionals, teachers, and parents must work together closely to diagnose and treat ADHD.

[Diagnosis Versus Assessment]

When a person is being observed for possible ADHD, health care providers often talk about "conducting an assessment" rather than looking for a diagnosis.

Diagnosis is a process of identifying an illness or disorder. By contrast, assessments are designed to evaluate all possible causes of a problem and determine specific approaches to improve the symptoms. Point of view is an important consideration, too. Diagnosis focuses on the negative aspects of a disorder—on how it causes problems for the person. Assessments look for evidence of a child's skills and strengths, especially those that can be used to offset symptoms. And perhaps most important, assessments serve to determine whether there is more than one cause for the symptoms, so that all causes can be treated.

Medical Doctors

Visiting the child's usual pediatrician or family practice doctor initially offers some important benefits. The doctor often has a few years of medical records to look back on. Also, the doctor may be familiar with the child's family situation and the health histories of parents and siblings. If the child is seeing a new doctor for the initial ADHD assessment, as much of this background information as possible will be gathered. A medical doctor's first approach is usually to rule out physical causes for unusual behavior.

In the exam, the doctor will probably ask about changes at home or in school that might have created stress. The doctor will work with the parents to review behaviors from younger stages in the child's life, since earlier signs of ADHD might have been overlooked. Information about how the child has been sleeping and eating recently can be revealing as well. Problems with eating or sleeping can be symptoms of ADHD but can also reflect illness or depression.

Repeated ear infections or hearing loss can cause children to appear inattentive and to experience learning difficulties.

When it's uncertain whether a child has ADHD, some physicians may recommend a drug trial. This involves administering a common ADHD-treatment drug—usually a stimulant such as Ritalin—and then observing the child over a short period of time. The assumption is that a child with ADHD will experience a reduction of symptoms in response to the medication. The problem with this approach is that many other disorders are related to ADHD and show similar symptoms. This may cause the child to be misdiagnosed.

Tests that measure how well a person can reason and learn new information are often helpful when trying to determine if someone has ADHD.

[ADHD Professionals]

As you begin your evaluation for ADHD, you will
probably see a therapist (a counselor or psychologist)
or a psychiatrist (a medical doctor who specializes in
mental and emotional disorders). These specialists can
test you for ADHD by observing your behavior and
administering detailed tests. Therapists and psychiatrists
can help you make plans to deal with your particular
challenges and help you talk through your frustrations.
Psychiatrists are also able to prescribe medications to
treat your symptoms.

Social workers may become involved as well. They talk
with you and your family and observe you in your home,
to uncover all of the factors that might help or hinder
your treatment. For example, the social worker may
gather details about your health history, look at how the
people in your home get along, and review your school
records. In one-on-one sessions with you, social
workers can also help you deal with family, social, and
school problems.

Mental Health Professionals

Psychologists, psychiatrists, and neurologists (medical doctors who specialize in the nervous system) are also critical to the assessment process. Therapists are very much involved, too. They are trained to look for signs of mental and emotional disorders. To get a full picture of the situation, parents, teachers, and other adults are asked to fill out questionnaires that can help clarify symptoms. The therapist may offer some toys or games to play with and may ask the child to explain how he or she would act in particular situations. All of this activity is designed to help the therapist understand the child's feelings, responses, and skills. A wide variety of tests may be administered during this part of an assessment.[2]

Although tests may be time-consuming and you may find them frustrating or repetitive, they can provide mental health professionals with a wider, more accurate understanding of your symptoms and skills.

The Continuous Performance Test (CPT) is one such test. During a CPT, the child is placed in front of a computer screen and instructed to respond in particular ways to the images that come up. For example, the child may be asked to click the return key every time a picture of a house is shown, and *not* to click when the letter X comes up. (This sounds easy until you actually see the test happening—the images zip by at a rapid-fire pace, and it takes a lot of attention and self-control to resist clicking the return key automatically!) The accuracy of responses in a CPT can provide some information about how well the child's nervous system filters images and how much control the child has over his or her responses.[3]

Kids who may have ADHD are also asked to take a close look at their own behaviors and rate them on evaluative scales.[4] The Diagnostic Interview for Children and Adolescents (DICA-IV) is a survey that asks a series of questions related to the DSM criteria. Any child who can read at a fourth-grade level can take the DICA-IV. The Conners-Wells Adolescent Self-Report Scale serves a similar purpose but is designed for children in middle school or above. It contains eighty-seven questions broken down into specific categories related to learning, behavior, emotions, and family relationships.

Along the way, psychologists must also look at the child's educational experience and skills. They often start by reviewing school records, including the results of standardized tests that are given in certain grades. The Wechsler Individual Achievement Test (WIAT) is often used to determine students' ability to read, write, express themselves verbally, listen, and solve number or logic problems. And although ADHD does not affect intelligence, routine intelligence tests (called IQ tests) are given to determine the child's overall ability to learn information and put it to use.

Tests of attention, memory, response time, and ability to do fine-motor tasks are normal parts of ADHD assessment. They help medical professionals determine which parts of your brain might be involved in causing symptoms. Some children might be tested to see how well they can control their emotions, while others are asked to organize thoughts and objects and to recall things they have recently seen, done, or been told about. It is also important to determine how children perceive themselves (self-confident or insecure, smart or unintelligent, outgoing or shy, etc.).

Parents and Teachers

Psychologists also need to know how children behave at home and at school. Family relationships are often affected by ADHD—and on the flip side, ADHD and other mental health issues can be made worse when there is conflict at home. Several surveys, including the Conflict Behavior Questionnaire and the ADHD Behavior Checklist, are designed to clarify how families interact.[5]

Parents may take special versions of the DICA-IV or the Conners survey so that their results can be compared to the child's. Extra questions are added to the parent surveys, providing information on the mother's health and behavior during pregnancy

Psychologists need to know how someone interacts with others at home and at school in order to determine if he or she has ADHD.

and how the birth went. Parents are also asked to describe the child's early years—when the child met certain milestones (such as crawling, holding objects between two fingers, and talking), how the child behaved in particular situations (such as when left with a babysitter or first placed in a preschool class), and so on. Both tests have built-in "red flag" questions—meaning questions that provide important clues to events that might have caused ADHD.

Red flags include issues such as a mother's use of alcohol during pregnancy, a premature birth, a history of family thyroid disease, exposure to particular chemicals, childhood malnutrition, and an early childhood head injury.

"Eight percent of White non-Hispanic children, five percent of Black non-Hispanic children, and nearly four percent of Hispanic children were reported to have ADHD."

— U.S. Environmental Protection Agency[6]

Other surveys ask teachers to rate students on how they solve problems (social or academic) at school and on their ability to adapt to particular challenges. The Behavioral Assessment System for Children (BASC) and the Behavior Disorders Identification Scale (BDIS) are tools commonly used to gather such information from teachers. Separate scales exist to determine whether the student has learning disabilities.[7]

Identifying the complete picture of a person's physical, mental, and neurological condition is the key to helping that person become healthy and productive. Once this picture becomes clear, it is easier to identify which treatments will work best. ADHD treatment takes many forms. For young people, it often involves one or more medications, therapy, and preparation of learning plans that will improve their ability to succeed at school.

Some of the tests psychologists use to help diagnose ADHD may be a lot like puzzles and games you have played at home or school.

Because several other disorders have symptoms that are similar to ADHD, it's important for doctors and therapists to check for all possible problems. And even when ADHD is clearly diagnosed, other disorders may accompany it and complicate the symptoms. A wide variety of **comorbidities** (illnesses, diseases, or disorders that accompany another health problem) are associated with ADHD. Some of these are medical conditions; others are psychological.

Psychological comorbidities that may accompany ADHD include learning disabilities, clinical depression and bipolar disorder, anxiety, conduct disorder, and oppositional-defiant disorder.

Depression is one of the least common comorbidities with ADHD.[8]

At least one in five kids with ADHD also has learning disabilities.[9] These occur when the person has difficulty with reading, writing, calculating numbers, or other basic skills that are involved in everyday learning. A large proportion of people with ADHD have trouble with handwriting (dysgraphia), for example, and many of them read below their grade level. Kids with ADHD are too frequently labeled as underachievers, especially if they have not been diagnosed. But there is no scientific evidence that either ADHD or learning disabilities affect intelligence.

Most of us experience some degree of depression when our lives become overly stressful or during episodes of ill health. This type of depression usually passes in a short time. Clinical depression, however, does not. Clinically depressed people go through extended bouts of sadness, hopelessness, guilt, and fatigue. They may have trouble sleeping or eating and can even find it difficult to get out of the house to go to work or school. In severe cases, depression can lead to suicidal thoughts or actions.

(continued on next page)

Bipolar disorder is another form of depression. Kids with bipolar disorder show symptoms that, on the surface, may be confused with hyperactive/impulsive-type ADHD. It's possible to distinguish between the two using two specific characteristics: how the child behaves during normal play and the rate at which the child speaks. In general, hyperactive children play calmly unless stressed, and they speak at a normal rate. Those with bipolar disorder tend to play and speak at an accelerated rate much of the time. Physicians and therapists must pay careful attention when distinguishing between the two disorders. They must also be on the lookout for the possibility that a patient has both.

Like depression, a bit of anxiety can be a normal part of life. But it can also be the result of a neurological disorder. The clinical form of anxiety is referred to as generalized anxiety disorder (GAD). GAD causes sufferers to go through the day with a nagging sense that things are going to go wrong. They worry about their actions, about what others will think of them, about what will happen in school, and about their health. This last worry is made worse by the fact that physical symptoms often occur with anxiety, including shortness of breath, headaches, exhaustion, sweating, and difficulty sleeping.

Conduct disorder causes people to show excessive anger and destructiveness. It may lead them to lie, cheat, steal, set fires, harm animals or people, and generally behave in ways that are considered antisocial. One-quarter of people with ADHD may also be diagnosed with conduct disorder. Related to this is oppositional-defiant disorder (ODD), which can affect up to one-third of all people with ADHD.[10] It causes children to be disobedient, hostile to others (especially to adults who have authority over them), and stubborn; they don't usually break laws, however, or physically harm others. Some researchers recognize two levels of ODD. One is mild, with symptoms tending to disappear by adulthood. This version is more common in females. Males tend to show symptoms of a more severe form of ODD, which appears before middle school and continues into adulthood.

Medical conditions can also occur with ADHD and complicate its symptoms. Tourette's syndrome is a genetic disorder that causes **tics**, or habitual movements a person cannot control. Tics often take the form of involuntary physical movements such as jerking or hitting; they may also be spoken, taking the form of grunts, repeated statements, shouts, or curses. While Tourette's isn't common, about half of those who experience the syndrome also have ADHD.[11]

At least one in four people with ADHD experiences GAD as well.[12]

chapter 3

Causes of ADHD

In the past, ADHD was blamed on everything from brain injuries, poor parenting, and ineffective teaching to just plain naughtiness on the part of children. Today, medical experts know that ADHD is a medical disorder of the brain. But how does the brain function, and what's different about the brains of people with ADHD? Scientists are still figuring those questions out.

In a computer, wired circuits tell different parts of the machine how to behave. In the human body, the brain acts something like a computer. Nerve cells, or **neurons**, are special cells that act like electrical circuits by transmitting information throughout the body. Like most

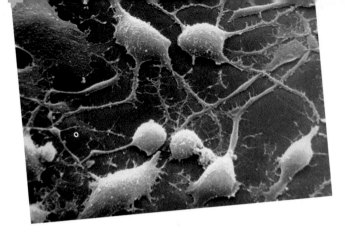

The largest neuron in the body is only 0.004 inches (0.1 millimeter) wide.

other cells in the human body, neurons are too small to see with the naked eye.

Unlike most body cells, however, neurons have long extensions, called fibers, that stretch away from the main part, or body, of the cell. Your brain and spinal cord contain billions of nerve cells, each with many fibers reaching out to different parts of your body.

There are two different categories of fibers attached to nerve cells: axons and dendrites. Each neuron has a single, long axon, which carries signals away from the cell. It also has one or more branching dendrites, which receive nerve **impulses** from nearby nerve cells. Axons may be as little as a fraction of an inch long, or they may reach as much as 3 feet (1 meter) in length. The average human brain contains as many as one hundred billion neurons, which serve to transmit signals between different parts of the brain and to the rest of the body.

Although the brain is considered a single organ, the brain is actually divided into many parts that perform distinct functions.[1] These parts are located in three major regions: the cerebrum, the cerebellum, and the brain stem. The whole brain is protected from injury by a thick cap of bone—the skull.

The brain of an adult human weighs about 3 pounds (1.4 kilograms) and accounts for roughly 2 percent of total body weight.

Cerebrum

The cerebrum is the largest part of the brain. It is involved in thinking, decision making, and memory. The cerebrum also receives messages from nerves around the body, controlling the ability to see, smell, hear, touch, and taste. The surface layer of the cerebrum, called the cerebral cortex (Latin for "bark"), is folded and twisted. No more than one-fifth of an inch (5 mm) thick, the cortex contains most of the brain's nerve cell bodies.

The cerebrum is divided, from front to back, into right and left halves, or hemispheres. And although these hemispheres don't appear to have distinct parts, decades of medical research have made it clear that different regions of the cortex play very different roles. Five lobes (the scientific term

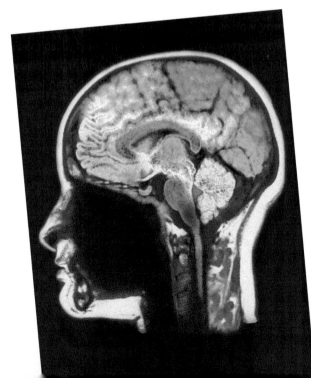

for these regions) have been identified in the cerebral cortex:

- The lobes located directly behind your forehead are called the frontal lobes. They control the executive functions (decision making and the ability to reason, argue, plan, organize, write, and speak). Emotions and impulses are also controlled here. This part of the brain helps you sort through all the information your senses collect. The frontal lobes help you prioritize what's important in your environment and "tune out" everything else. They also make it possible for you to delay your responses slightly, improving the chances that your reactions are appropriate to the situation. Studies conducted in 2003 at the University of California at Los Angeles (UCLA) showed that people with ADHD tend to have slightly smaller frontal lobes, which accounts for many of the symptoms related to attention, impulsivity, and difficulties with organization and time management.[2] Reduced blood flow to the frontal regions may also contribute to hyperactivity.[3]

- Behind the frontal lobes, at the top of the head, are the parietal lobes. They maintain the senses of taste, smell, and touch and are responsible for your awareness of pain and temperature.

- At the back of the skull are the occipital lobes, which control vision and make connections between things we see now and related memories.

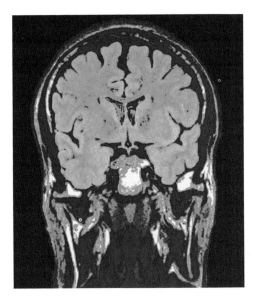

The left side of the brain
is generally associated
with skills in language,
computing numbers,
science, and reasoning.
The right brain handles
creative and artistic
functions and the ability
to imagine.

- A fourth pair of lobes is located on the sides of the head, behind your ears. These temporal lobes are the source of your ability to hear and understand language. The 2003 study at UCLA also showed size reductions in this part of the brain for people with ADHD, which may impact attention.

- Tucked into the space between the temporal lobes and the frontal lobes are the insula. The job of this fifth pair of lobes is to manage functions of the brain stem (described below).

Deep within the lobes is a group of small organs that help parts of the brain communicate with each other. Researchers at Harvard University's McLean Hospital have shown that one of these parts—the putamen—does not receive as much blood flow in people with ADHD.[4]

The same lobes in each hemisphere can—and usually do—act independently of each other. This built-in ability to "multitask" makes it possible for your brain to control many functions at once. The hemispheres exchange information through a thick band of nerves called the corpus callosum. This region is smaller in people with ADHD, which impacts memory and higher-order thinking (the ability to make connections between ideas and to see "the big picture").

Cerebellum

A second major region of the brain, the cerebellum, is located below the occipital lobes of the cerebrum and consists of two masses of tissue. The cerebellum controls movements of the body, particularly balance and coordination. Memories of how to do complex movements such as walking, typing, or riding a bicycle are also stored here. This part of the brain changes extremely rapidly during adolescence. The cerebellum is about 6 percent smaller in people with ADHD, but it is not yet clear what role this plays in causing symptoms.[5]

> The cerebellum looks a lot like a head of cauliflower that's been cut in half.

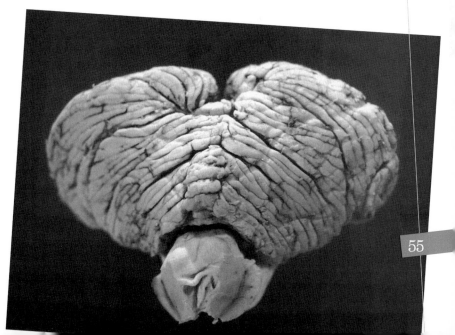

Brain Stem

The brain stem is housed between the halves of the cerebellum. This deep location serves a practical purpose: the brain stem is responsible for many of the body's life functions, including heart rate and breathing, so it requires extra protection from injury. The spinal cord (a band of nerve fibers extending down the back of the body) begins here, and the brain stem coordinates communications between the body, the spinal cord, and the brain.

Neurotransmitters and ADHD

Much of the time, individual nerve cells are at rest: no signal is moving through them. Neurons are activated (or "fired") by some kind of stimulation, such as light, heat, or pressure. This stimulation causes an electrical signal or impulse to flow along the nerve's axon with incredible speed—as fast as 366 feet per second (112 m per second). When the impulse reaches the end of an axon, it must move across an open space, called a **synapse**, in order to reach the next neuron and continue on its path. If the impulse does not make this jump, no message is carried to the appropriate part of the brain or body.

A serious complication exists, however: electrical impulses cannot cross the fluid-filled synapse. The nervous system solves this problem by storing the energy of electrical impulses inside chemical molecules called **neurotransmitters**. These chemicals can pass through the nerve cell membrane and move across the synapse toward neighboring nerve cells. When a neurotransmitter molecule reaches another nerve cell, it "docks" on that cell's surface. Docking sites are called **receptors**, and each is like a keyhole into which only one kind of neurotransmitter "key" fits.

Once a neurotransmitter has docked, its receptor opens inward (toward the inside of the nerve cell). Here the neurotransmitter's energy once again becomes an electrical signal. It can either "excite" the nerve—stimulating it to carry the signal on—or "inhibit" the cell, causing it to stop or slow its actions. The more molecules of a given neurotransmitter that are involved in this process, the more effective the signal transmission is. After completing their task, neurotransmitters either return to the axon for reuse or are broken down by other chemicals in the synapse.

The human body produces more than sixty different types of neurotransmitter chemicals, and at least five of these are directly involved in causing the symptoms of ADHD (see Table 1).[6]

Table 1.
Neurotransmitters involved in producing ADHD-related symptoms

Neurotransmitter
Dopamine
Serotonin
Norepinephrine (also called noradrenaline)
Epinephrine
GABA (gamma-amino butyric acid)

In normal amounts, dopamine helps a person's brain block out distractions, controls behavior, coordinates movement of the body, and produces emotions related to pleasure or pain. Dopamine sometimes works to shut off or block supplies of other neurotransmitters.	Low levels of dopamine cause electrical signals in the nervous system to move more slowly or stop completely. In turn, this affects the brain's ability to manage executive functions. Coordination and memory are also reduced.
Affects moods, sleep, and the awareness of pain. Also regulates body temperature and controls a person's urge to eat.	The exact impact on ADHD is not yet understood, but low levels of serotonin in the body can cause depression and make it hard to sleep.
Regulates emotions and attentiveness, and influences dreams. It can also sometimes stop the effects of other neurotransmitters.	Deficiencies reduce the ability to pay attention and focus, and may cause anxiety.
Affects how the body uses sugars for nutrition and energy. Also controls the heart rate.	Low levels contribute to inattention.
Inhibits the effects of other neurotransmitters.	Low levels of GABA can affect coordination, movement, and vision.

[Genetics and ADHD]

The role of **genetics** in ADHD is important. One-third of all children with ADHD have family members who also have the disorder.[7] In other words, ADHD is usually inherited from parents, the same way we inherit traits such as eye and hair color. If you can roll your tongue, have a cleft (dimple) in your chin, or if you go bald as an adult, you inherited those traits from your biological parents.

All traits are carried on **chromosomes**. These long strands of protein are found inside the nucleus of every cell in the body. On each chromosome, there are specific regions that control particular parts of the body's growth, development, and functioning. These are called **genes**.

"Thirty to forty percent of children diagnosed with ADHD have relatives with the same type of problem."

—National Mental Health Association[8]

[Environmental Causes of ADHD]

Although genetics is probably the main cause of ADHD, the disorder can sometimes be caused by environmental factors—things that happen to people during their lifetime. Several studies have made a connection between ADHD and a mother's use of drugs, alcohol, or tobacco during pregnancy. Because an unborn child (also called a fetus) shares a blood supply with its mother, the fetus is exposed to any chemical substance that goes into the mother's bloodstream. Frequent contact with such materials may cause the fetus's brain to develop poorly. This, in turn, can result in ADHD during childhood.

Two types of chemical toxins have also been linked to ADHD: lead and polychlorinated biphenyls (PCBs).[9]

Lead was once used as an ingredient in house paint. In the 1960s, it was discovered that high levels of lead might cause learning disabilities in children and make them hyperactive, inattentive, and disruptive. Because of this, the United States Consumer Product Safety Commission (CPSC) decided to set limits to the amount of lead that could be used in manufacturing. (The CPSC is a federal government agency established to ensure that the products made and purchased by Americans are not hazardous to their health.) In 1978, the CPSC passed a law limiting the amount of lead that could be used in any product. But even today, some old buildings still contain lead-based paints, which pose a health risk to pregnant mothers, fetuses, and young children.[10]

(continued on next page)

PCBs were once used as insulation in industrial and commercial buildings. These highly toxic chemicals got into many of America's waterways when industries dumped their wastes. In 1976, PCBs were banned in the United States.[11] Yet, like lead, PCBs remain in the environment for decades. They can be found in the bodies of fish—particularly in the Great Lakes. When a pregnant mother eats this contaminated fish, the PCBs can pass through her bloodstream to her fetus. Babies can also be exposed to PCBs through breast milk. Instead of passing out of the body as a waste, these chemicals are stored in fat cells. They can cause problems with the brain development of children, reducing their ability to learn and causing hyperactivity.

Premature birth may be another reason that ADHD develops. Children who weighed less than 3.3 pounds (1.5 kg) at birth are especially at risk. Their brains are not completely developed when they are born. Once born, the infant's body must focus on survival rather than growth. As a result, the brain may never reach its full size. A study conducted in England during the 1990s showed that 26 percent of extremely premature children were later diagnosed with ADHD.[12]

Although physicians and researchers now recognize that ADHD is a medical condition in the brain, the causes are still being explored. Theories state that the condition could be caused by one single trigger or a combination of several. Regardless of what started it, however, once ADHD has been recognized, it is time to find a way to treat it—and learn to live with it.

Part two:
Living Well with
ADHD

chapter 4

Treatment Options

Like other disorders that are caused (at least in part) by chemical imbalances, such as migraine headaches and depression, ADHD cannot be cured. Patients sometimes seem to outgrow these disorders as they mature. In the meantime, however, treatment is often needed to ease symptoms (see Table 2).

The decision to take medications for treatment of ADHD symptoms remains controversial. If you are diagnosed with ADHD, your family must base this decision on a variety of factors. You may find that medication is unavoidable because symptoms are so severe that they interfere with your ability to learn or get along with others. In that case, medication could be a good, short-term solution until you learn new behaviors that can improve your symptoms. Most experts agree that the best treatment for ADHD includes a combination of medication, therapy, and behavioral training. Alternatively, your parents may decide that medication is not an option—they may prefer to help you find other ways of coping.

Medications

Once the decision is made to medicate, there are many options to choose from. When making a recommendation, your doctor takes into account which symptoms are most troublesome for you. The presence of comorbid conditions also influences the choice. Five major categories of medication are currently used to treat ADHD: stimulants, antidepressants, antianxiety drugs, antihypertensives, and selective norepinephrine reuptake inhibitors (SNRIs).

Stimulants

In 1937, Dr. Charles Bradley was working at a Rhode Island hospital that specialized in children with behavioral disorders. He discovered that half the children behaved better and did better work at school when he gave them Benzedrine.[1] (Benzedrine is a stimulant that was originally developed to treat sinus congestion.) Another type of stimulant drug, called methylphenidate, was released in 1956. Its brand name is familiar to many people today: Ritalin. In the past few decades, several other brands of methylphenidate have been developed, including

Focalin, Metadate, and Concerta. **Amphetamines** like Dexedrine and Adderall are also used.

Scientists are still trying to figure out exactly why stimulants improve ADHD symptoms. The best evidence suggests that they increase levels of neurotransmitters in the brain, particularly **dopamine**. This might be because the medication prevents transporter molecules from recycling neurotransmitters so fast. Then again, the stimulant might actually increase the production of neurotransmitters.

When they work, stimulants increase your ability to focus. Dramatic emotional outbursts tend to decrease, and you feel calmer. Children who usually experience clumsiness as part of their symptoms will often find that they are more in control of their bodies. Stimulants also seem to make people with ADHD get along better with others.

Stimulant drugs work for about 70 to 80 percent of all people with attention-deficit disorders.[2] They are less effective for those with inattentive-type ADHD.

Each brand of stimulant has slighty different effects. Also, most of the brands have varieties that last for different amounts of time. Your schedule and specific goals determine which brand and which duration are best for you.

Despite the successes of stimulants, there are some concerns that your family must consider. For example, some stimulant users experience tics (involuntary bodily movements). Your doctor may address this by lowering the dosage or by trying another medication entirely. There have also been some indications that children may stop growing while on stimulants. The reasons behind this apparent slowdown in growth are still unclear. But experts say that the body will make up the growth at later points in the child's development.

Some families decide to stop giving their children ADHD medication during school holidays. Called a "medication vacation," it gives the child's body a chance to rest and grow.

[Controversy: Are Stimulants Addictive?]

Used according to prescription, stimulant drugs should never pose a danger of addiction. However, if taken in large doses, they may cause uncomfortable increases in anxiety and hyperactivity (just the opposite effect they are prescribed to prevent). Also, stimulants are generally given as a pill that gradually breaks down in the intestines, releasing the dosage slowly into the body. When these pills are abused—for example, crushed and then swallowed—the body absorbs the drug very rapidly. Dopamine levels in the brain increase too quickly, and using stimulants this way may increase a person's risk of trying other addictive drugs.

The risks of abuse or overdose provide a good argument for monitoring a young person's prescriptions. In addition to the risk of skipped doses or overuse, some kids also find that they can make money by selling stimulant pills to classmates. People who don't have ADHD find that the drug makes them more alert and able to study better for longer periods of time. They are willing to pay for this effect. Selling the drug is illegal, of course, in part because it holds the risk of causing harm to the buyer. Some non-ADHD people experience violent headaches after taking stimulants. There is also a risk of stroke, seizure, and even death.

Antidepressants

Antidepressants are the second major category of ADHD treatment drugs. These may be prescribed if you respond poorly (or not at all) to stimulants. True to their name, antidepressants can help you deal with the symptoms of anxiety and depression that sometimes accompany ADHD. They can be an excellent choice if you have inattentive-type ADHD. They improve your ability to handle those complex executive functions—organization and planning, reasoning and emotional control, transitioning, and short-term memory—and along the way will increase motivation. Some people find that they also sleep better when using these drugs.

Antianxiety Drugs

Antianxiety drugs work in a way that is opposite to stimulants—they reduce the levels of GABA (gamma-amino butyric acid), a neurotransmitter that slows down the rate at which your nerves fire. People who experience severe hyperactivity are better able to relax when taking antianxiety drugs.

> "ADD is like going through life carrying a one man band contraption, with a broken strap."
>
> —Julia Smith-Ruetz[3]

Antihypertensives

Antihypertensives improve symptoms of hyperactivity, impulsivity, and aggression—but they will not be helpful if you experience inattention. The two types of antihypertensives can be given together through a patch that is attached to your skin; this allows the drugs to release slowly and constantly. These drugs are often prescribed for patients who suffer tics when taking stimulants; the antihypertensive tends to reduce the effect of the stimulant.

SNRIs

The newest category of ADHD drugs is the SNRI (selective norepinephrine reuptake inhibitor). Unlike stimulants, which seem to increase dopamine levels directly, SNRIs work by controlling the balance of another neurotransmitter, norepinephrine, which in turn regulates dopamine levels. The results are similar to those of stimulants: increased attention span, more ability to organize, and better impulse control.

Table 2. Categories of medication used to treat ADHD

Category
Stimulant: Methylphenidate
Stimulant: Amphetamine
Antidepressant
Antidepressant: Selective Serotonin Reuptake Inhibitor (SSRI)
Antidepressant: Tricyclic
Antianxiety
Antihypertensive
Selective Norepinephrine Reuptake Inhibitor (SNRI)

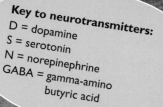

Key to neurotransmitters:
D = dopamine
S = serotonin
N = norepinephrine
GABA = gamma-amino
butyric acid

Brand names (not a complete list)	Duration of dose	Neurotransmitters affected	Effect on ADHD symptoms
Ritalin . . . . 4 hours Ritalin SR . . . . 6 hours Ritalin LA . . . . 8 hours Metadate . . . . 4 hours Metadate ER. . . . . 8 hours Metadate CD . . . . 8 hours Focalin . . . . 4 hours Concerta . . . . 12 hours		D	Prescribed to improve motor control and reduce hyperactivity and impulsivity
Dexedrine . . . . 4 hours Dexedrine Spansules . . . . 8 hours Adderall . . . . .14 hours Adderall XR . . . . 12 hours		S,N	Prescribed to improve motor control and reduce hyperactivity and impulsivity
Wellbutrin-SR . . . . 8 hours Wellbutrin-XL . . . . . Taken once daily		N,D	Prescribed to relieve depression and anxiety and improve motivation
Prozac Lexapro Zoloft Paxil	Taken once daily	S	Prescribed to provide relief from symptoms of depression and improve ability to sleep
Norpramin	Taken once daily	S,N	Prescribed to relieve tics, especially in cases where stimulants are ineffective; also to treat depression
Klonopin Ativan	8–12 hours	GABA	Prescribed to slow down the nervous system, and help the body relax
Catapres Tenex	8–12 hours in pill form; continuous in patch	N	Prescribed to treat tics; best used in combination with a methylphenidate stimulant
Strattera	6–8 hours	N,D	Prescribed to reduce inattention, hyperactivity, and impulsivity

73

[Why So Many Versions of the Same Drugs?]

It might seem odd that several ADHD medications are available in different forms. Over time, as drug manufacturers have continued to test well-known ADHD drugs, they have created versions that act somewhat differently. Doctors can now prescribe a drug that not only deals with each patient's particular symptoms, but also matches the person's lifestyle. Some patients need only a few hours of coverage to get them through classes. Some respond better when taking the drug two or three times a day. Others prefer a lasting dose so they don't have to remember to take pills later in the day. Ritalin, Metadate, Adderall, and many other drugs offer varieties with short- and long-acting effects.

Finding the Right Medication

It may take several tries to find a medication, or combination of medications, that works for you. In the long run, the goal is to find a brand that relieves your symptoms with the lowest possible dose.[4]

You, and all the other people in your life, need to be patient as you go through this process—it can take time for the full effects of a particular drug to kick in (or for it to become clear that a medication will not be right for you). You may also find that a medication eventually stops working, even if it was great for a long time. This is not unusual among teenagers and

While going through a drug trial, people often find that it helps them—and the medical professionals involved in their care—to keep a daily journal noting when the medication was taken, how it made them feel at different times through the day, and any side effects.

young adults, because the chemistry of their bodies is changing as they grow and mature.

Every medication has side effects, though some are more obvious than others. Headache, dizziness, and grumpiness may occur with stimulants. Antidepressants and antihypertensives can make you feel "spaced out" or sleepy. Some kids on antidepressants also become constipated or dizzy. With most ADHD medications, side effects occur for only a few hours; they fade as the dose gradually leaves the body. (Doses of antidepressants are an exception to this rule. They are designed to remain at a constant level in the body, so side effects can be a lasting problem.) Fortunately, in many cases, side effects lessen or disappear once the body adjusts to a new medication.[5]

One problem that sometimes occurs with stimulant use is called **rebound**. This is a situation in which symptoms actually seem to worsen as the medication wears off. The best way to prevent rebound is to try a new medication.

[Ask Your Doctor]

As you try new medications, don't be shy about asking your doctor questions. Particularly when starting a new medication, you and your parents need clear instructions about how and when to take it. Some important questions include:

- Can you freely go off and on the medication (for example, choosing to take more before a big test or less on the weekends)?
- What positive and negative side effects should you look for?
- Will you experience any personality changes?
- Do you need to avoid any other medications (such as prescribed antibiotics if you get an infection)?

[Using Your Medications Responsibly]

Taking a medication requires a certain level of responsibility—especially if you want to be in charge of your own doses. As a result, there are some rules that must be followed:

- Never decrease, increase, or stop your medication dosage without consulting your doctor. This includes taking "medication vacations" during weekends, holidays, and summer breaks.
- Never take any kind of prescription drug unless it has been prescribed for you directly by a doctor—and check with your parents before taking over-the-counter medications.
- It's both dangerous—and illegal!—to share (or sell) your prescription medications with others. Giving your medications to other people can literally put their lives at risk.
- If the medication doesn't work or causes uncomfortable side effects, talk with your doctor about options.

Loss of appetite can be a real concern for some stimulant users. Taking the drug with, or very shortly before, a meal can usually prevent this problem. If this doesn't work, eating frequent small meals may be effective. If you experience severe appetite loss, your doctor will probably recommend altering the dose or switching to another medication in the same category. Stomachaches can also occur shortly after taking some medications. To reduce this, try eating a few dry crackers and drinking a full glass of water when taking the dose.

Insomnia (difficulty sleeping) is another problem for many people with ADHD. Ideally, medications can help relieve this symptom. In some cases, however, medications may have no effect or may make the problem worse (particularly among stimulant users). A change in medication is one option in these cases. Reducing the dose of stimulant drugs taken in the afternoon can be a practical way to avoid insomnia at bedtime. A small dose of stimulant, given right at bedtime, slightly increases the levels of neurotransmitters in the brain, which eases symptoms and helps you relax for sleep.

Beyond Medications

On bad days, it can feel terribly frustrating to have ADHD. At times like these, it's important to remember that you can make a big difference in how ADHD affects your life. Taking prescribed medications regularly is a critical step in controlling symptoms for some people. But while medications may relieve your symptoms, they don't give you an immediate, magical ability to do things you never learned to do. For example, you need to find ways to talk productively with the people in your life so that all your feelings aren't trapped inside. You also may have missed the chance to learn some social, emotional, or academic skills in the years before your ADHD was diagnosed.

Most experts recommend that people with ADHD create a comprehensive treatment plan—one that includes psychological therapy and behavioral therapy in addition to medication. (A learning plan designed to meet your educational needs is also recommended; this is discussed in the next chapter.)

There are many options for treatment plans. Psychological therapy can be done individually, with your family, or in groups that include other kids. Some behavioral training might take place in these sessions, but it can also be done with trained coaches or more informally with your family.

Counseling

It's not uncommon for people with ADHD to experience feelings of anger, anxiety, frustration, or fear as a result of their challenges. You may think of yourself as a failure or a misfit—then again, you may feel great about yourself but frustrated with people who expect you to behave differently. The point of therapy is for you to have someone in your life who can help you

Remember that what you discuss with your therapist is private, so you can be honest with your thoughts and take risks that no one else necessarily has to know about. However, medical professionals are also legally obligated to protect you and others, which means they can talk to your family if they feel you are likely to hurt yourself or anyone else.

work through these issues and help you find ways to resolve conflicts.

Good therapists probably won't give you easy answers to the problems you bring up. Instead, they should guide you toward insights that reveal why your behaviors happen. Therapists can also give you some tools to get through challenging moments in your life. For example, they may teach you relaxation techniques to help reduce stress and anxiety. You might do role-playing activities that help you practice dealing with difficult situations. All this work is geared toward making you feel better from day to day and helping your life run more smoothly in general.

There may be times when the therapist suggests that you meet together with your family. (You can ask for this kind of session, too.) Such meetings ensure that your parents have the information they need to help you and that they become aware if your therapy is not working well. The therapist may even recommend family meetings regularly if you need extra support or if family issues are a core part of the problem.

Group therapy is another type of counseling situation. It puts you together with a therapist and a number of other people who have similar concerns, challenges, or goals. Group therapy might sound silly to you at first. It might seem intimidating to share your feelings with strangers. But it can be a great way to share ideas and get helpful feedback—and, perhaps most important, it's a great reminder that you are not alone. Lots of kids have ADHD, and by sharing your experiences in therapy, you can sometimes help each other.

Support Groups

Support groups are just what their name implies: a group of people getting together to encourage each other through some situation. These meetings are usually less formal than group therapy, and there is no counselor in charge—members run the meetings. This may mean that meetings become more social than therapeutic, but that can be a great benefit if the members don't experience conflict or get distracted from the goal of supporting one another. Local community centers sometimes have information about support groups. Check with your therapist as well. You may even find that your school has an organization that focuses on ADHD or learning disabilities.

[Establishing Goals]

Whether you work with a coach, a counselor, or just sit down to plan with your family, some of the goals of behavioral therapy for kids with ADHD can include:

- finding productive ways to deal with bullies (or to control your own pushy tendencies)
- learning to talk in healthy ways with the people in your life
- creating systems to organize your belongings
- identifying methods for managing your schedule so you can get places on time and be more efficient
- figuring out how to break large projects and goals into small tasks that seem less daunting
- establishing "contracts"—agreements between you and other people (teachers, parents, or even friends) that lay out specific actions you will do (or not do) in particular situations, as well as consequences and rewards
- setting goals for future accomplishments

Coaching and Behavioral Therapy

While regular therapy focuses on the emotional aspects of dealing with ADHD, behavioral therapy teaches the practical approaches you can take to resolve problems. It stresses the need for each individual to identify the behaviors that affect his or her health and well-being, and what work needs to be done to overcome those behaviors. This may involve finding new ways to structure your home or school environment, or using rewards and consequences to change behaviors in specific ways.

Behavioral therapy is sometimes done with an ADHD coach, whose job is to work closely with you to build skills that improve your life and learning. These solutions aren't always obvious, and it can benefit you and your family greatly to work with an expert, even for a short time, to uncover them. ADHD coaches can also work with you to build social skills. These skills can be difficult for kids with ADHD to understand, but they are essential for day-to-day success. After all, you will need to communicate with family, friends, teachers, and co-workers throughout your life. With the coach, you can practice conversations, learn to recognize people's moods and intentions, and figure out how to resolve conflicts.

ADHD affects the whole family, and for this reason parents may also want to undertake some behavioral therapy to help improve their own skills at organization, time management, conflict resolution, or communication.

Mental health professionals are beginning to understand the essential role that nature plays in keeping humans emotionally, psychologically, and physically healthy. In a study released in 2004, researchers at the University of Illinois came up with some intriguing results about the effect of nature and wild places on people with ADHD. They worked with a group of more than four hundred children who have ADHD, to see what kinds of free-time activities seemed to best improve symptoms.

Kids in the study were asked to write in a journal every day after they did certain kinds of relaxation activities in their free time outside school. The results were impressive and clear.

Kids who spent a lot of time indoors—even those who were engaged in educational activities such as games and puzzles—reported that their symptoms were basically unchanged after playing. Parents confirmed this, remarking that their children still had trouble following instructions and staying on task. Doing sports outside or playing on plastic-and-concrete playgrounds seemed to release excess energy for some of the kids, but it still didn't improve their symptoms greatly.

Children who spent more time outside in natural settings—in backyards with some plants, in undeveloped lots and fields, farms, or woods—were noticeably calmer and more focused in school and when doing homework.[6] They also interacted more productively with other people after "green therapy" sessions. The wilder the setting, the more improvement was shown.[7] ADHD experts from New York University have gotten similar results when testing kids in nature. Other researchers in the 1990s observed adults at their jobs. They found that those who could see greenery (if only just lawns) out the windows of their workplace were significantly more likely to be happy at work and to have a good attitude.[8]

chapter 5

ADHD and Learning

Intelligence and the urge to succeed are as strong in people with ADHD as in anyone else. But ADHD can put up some powerful barriers to learning that sometimes overcome "smarts" and "motivation": a tendency toward disorganization, disruptive behavior, and inattention are among these. Consequently, the quality of schoolwork may flip-flop from extremely detailed and insightful to sloppy and incomplete. Students with ADHD may find it hard to learn from their mistakes—and to avoid making them again—even when teachers provide detailed feedback.

[Some ADHD and School Statistics]

Statistics regarding ADHD and education are daunting. At least 20 percent of kids with ADHD have learning disabilities.[1] Half are likely to drop out or be expelled before graduating.[2] Those who leave school—either because they don't feel able to learn or because of social problems—are at a much higher risk of getting into trouble by running away from home, abusing drugs, or engaging in criminal activity. Preventing such situations should be the priority of all families and school systems. The experience and preparation kids get in high school are strong factors in how much they are able to accomplish later in life.

Learning Plans and Accommodations

In the United States, there are three federal laws designed to guarantee equal rights and equal access to education for all Americans. Similar laws have been passed in all states.

Section 504 of the Rehabilitation Act of 1973 was the first civil rights law to clearly define the responsibilities that public schools have in ensuring the success of all students.

In 1990, the Americans with Disabilities Act (ADA) made it law that students attending private schools should have the same rights as those attending public schools. The ADA and the Rehabilitation Act of 1973 prevent people with disabilities from being denied access to the same programs that nondisabled people can use.[3]

Under the Rehabilitation Act, a "504 plan" may be designed to keep you in regular classes, following the same schedule as your classmates and learning the same material. All the important adults in your life— family, counselors, teachers, learning specialists—work with you to design a plan that addresses the particular challenges you may face in a fast-paced classroom setting. The plan might include approval for getting additional time for taking tests or doing homework, sitting closer to the front of the classroom, taping classes or copying notes from classmates, or having an aide to help you stay organized.

Individualized Education Programs (IEPs) are a different kind of education plan and apply to

Some students with ADHD have an aide who helps them stay focused and organized at school.

students who have ADHD and other learning disorders. IEPs are covered under the Individuals with Disabilities Education Act (IDEA), which requires that all American schoolchildren have equal access to a high-quality, free education in public schools. IDEA differs from the Rehabilitation Act because it holds schools accountable for making available all the materials, funding, and other resources that students with disabilities—including ADHD—will need to complete their education.[4]

An IEP determines the services you will receive in school. These might include:

- regular visits to the school's learning specialist to learn study skills
- time with an occupational therapist, to work on improving physical coordination
- approval to visit the school counselor when you need advice or a chance to work through a problem
- tutoring to help you with homework
- an extra set of schoolbooks to keep at home
- transfer into a special education classroom for all or part of your day, so that you can get more personal attention and help with particular skills

An IEP should be adjusted over time—at least once a year—as your needs change. It also allows the school and your family to track your accomplishments over time.

Schools spend a lot of money to accommodate students with ADHD and other disabilities—as they should. But because it's expensive, you must provide proof of your disability from a doctor before a plan can be designed. IEPs are complicated and expensive to create, so they involve additional levels of testing before being written. This might include health testing (including hearing, vision, and speech), testing for learning disabilities and intelligence, a review of academic records, and an evaluation of social skills and emotional state. This is a long process, but it's worthwhile. It not only ensures that you get access to the specific assistance you need, but it can also help identify other issues (depression, learning disabilities, health problems) that accompany your ADHD and complicate your learning process.

"Sometimes a person with ADD feels as if their mind is moving as fast as a speeding train."

—Frank Coppola, MA, ODC, ACG (ADD Coach)[5]

[Maximizing Your Success at School]

School is a big part of every young person's life, and success there can go a long way toward building self-esteem—not to mention paving the way for what can be accomplished in later years. School staff members can—and must—help set up a plan that maximizes your skills and accommodates your limitations. In the long run, however, your success depends on your commitment.

Here are a few suggestions:[6]

- Have routines in place that can ease the strain of a busy school day. Getting up on time and eating a good breakfast is a great way to start. Better yet, get ready the night before: shower, choose clothes, repack your backpack and leave it by the door, and pack a lunch or tuck lunch money in a zippered pocket of your pack.
- Sit near the front of the class so you can see what's going on.
- Whenever possible, avoid sitting near students who will divert your attention from what's happening in class. Friends can be just as distracting as people you don't get along with.
- Use a planner! You've probably heard this a thousand times—but that's because it can really work.
- Establish a locker organization system early in the school year. Put in shelves, set up a color-coding system—whatever works for you. Then stick with it throughout the year.

- Find a "comfort zone" at school where you can retreat if you are getting overwhelmed.
- Use a computer to help you get work done more quickly and neatly—but limit yourself to the use of one computer program at a time to avoid distractions.
- When doing homework, set a time frame for each task, and set a timer to keep yourself on schedule. Break down large projects into smaller pieces to make them less daunting and more manageable. Give yourself permission to take short breaks after accomplishing each task—but keep them short and stay on track.
- Begin studying for tests several days in advance! Identify the topics that are most challenging for you and then review or practice them daily for several days. See your teacher or learning specialist for extra help on subjects that still don't make sense.

chapter 6

Healthful Habits

Every young person has to figure out how to stay healthy. Good nutrition, plenty of physical activity, a regular sleep schedule, and avoidance of dangerous habits (such as the use of drugs or driving too fast) can go a long way toward making life more enjoyable. For kids with ADHD, choosing a healthful lifestyle can be a key factor in reducing symptoms.

Diet and Nutrition

The role of vitamins and minerals in ADHD is still controversial, but it's worth reviewing. Some nutritionists think that deficiencies of zinc and fatty acids make

ADHD worse. Zinc is a mineral that is involved in the body's production of two neurotransmitters: serotonin and dopamine. It also contributes to the **metabolism** of fatty acids. The human body cannot make fatty acids—it must get them from food sources such as fish, walnuts, and canola oil—yet they are essential

The jury is still out on whether nutrition problems (those associated with foods, vitamins, and minerals) can cause ADHD. But one food that can be ruled out as a problem is sugar. Although hyperactive behavior in children was blamed on high-sugar diets for many decades in the twentieth century, it is now clear that sugar does not cause ADHD symptoms.[1]

"Two to three times more boys than girls are diagnosed with ADHD."

—U.S. Environmental Protection Agency[2]

to our health. When metabolized, fatty acids are used to make both dopamine and norepinephrine,[3] so a deficiency of fatty acids seems a likely culprit in causing ADHD symptoms. Scientists in Europe and the Middle East have been prescribing zinc in combination with stimulants since the 1980s and have seen improvement. Based on these results, researchers at Ohio State University are conducting tests that may lead to similar recommendations in the United States.[4]

Exercise

It can seem overwhelming to start an exercise program. You might dislike sports, or perhaps your schedule seems too full already. But studies clearly show that all people—not just those with ADHD—experience amazing benefits from being active and getting fit. This doesn't mean that you suddenly have to begin training for a triathlon or bench-pressing your weight. Instead, find a form of exercise that suits your personality and that you can realistically do several times a week.

Joining a sports team works for some people. They like the structure and the built-in social interaction. Talking a walk or a bike ride may suit others better. These activities provide quiet time to reflect and unwind while you work out. In addition to toning your body and releasing stress, exercise causes your body to release chemicals called endorphins, which just plain make you feel good. And you will be amazed at how getting fit builds your sense of confidence.

Sleep

Believe it or not, sleeping isn't all about what happens when you lie down in bed at night. Your ability to sleep well is actually closely tied to your overall mental and physical health. A healthful sleep routine often starts with physical activity in the afternoon to tire out your body. Finishing homework well before bedtime can also make it easier to fall asleep. If you try to work right up to bedtime, your mind may continue to chug along actively for a while afterward rather than settling down into rest mode. Along those same lines,

To get the most from your hours of sleep, have a regular schedule. Going to bed at the same time each night and getting up about the same time each morning promotes good sleep.

it's a good idea to avoid overstimulating activities (such as high-intensity computer games) close to bedtime.

Sleep deprivation can be dangerous. Short-term sleep deprivation causes distraction and irritability. People suffering from a lack of sleep begin to show short- and long-term memory loss—they can't recall things that just happened and may even lose their ability to remember information they have known for many years (such as the multiplication tables or familiar people's names). Excessive sleep loss also makes people more vulnerable to illness and infection. Eventually, the brain begins to react more slowly to stimuli, which can cause clumsiness. Lack of sleep can even lead to serious accidents, especially when the exhausted person drives.

The question is, how much sleep is required to keep the mind and body healthy? The answer varies somewhat from person to person, but there are guidelines that can be followed for each age group. In

By nature, many young people with ADHD are inclined to do things that are risky. Curiosity leads them to experiment with drugs, alcohol, and cigarettes at an early age. Kids who feel isolated from peers or family are at significantly greater risk. In these cases, kids might simply be looking for something to make them feel better. Isolated kids are also more likely to connect with other social outsiders who make drugs available and exert pressure to try them. It's an unfortunate reality that many unprescribed drugs temporarily relieve ADHD symptoms—and that can prove a powerful temptation to kids who do not respond well to other treatments or who do not have emotional support from family, friends, or health care providers.

(continued on next page)

Marijuana is one of the most common drugs that tempt kids who have ADHD. Not everyone who uses pot becomes addicted, but ADHD increases this risk. There are two real problems with using this drug. First, it acts on the parts of the brain that control memory, problem solving, and coordination—three areas that are already less developed in people with ADHD. Second, marijuana is often impure—it may be laced with any of a variety of substances that are far more dangerous.

Young people with ADHD are also significantly more likely to start smoking than kids without ADHD.[5] Stress might be partly responsible for this, but there are physiological reasons as well. Nicotine can bind to nerve receptors in the same places that dopamine can. When this happens, a smoker may experience a short-term calming effect. However, this short-term effect is offset by the long-term effects of nicotine addiction and life threatening smoking-related diseases.

Kids with ADHD are even more likely to abuse alcohol than marijuana. Up to 40 percent of high school kids with ADHD have tried alcohol, and many of them use it regularly.

general, school-aged children, until about age twelve, need nine to ten hours of sleep each night. Teens require about nine hours of sleep[6], and adults need at least eight.

Driving

The privilege of driving is something most teenagers look forward to. For kids with ADHD, however, there are a few risks that go beyond those faced by all young drivers. Even when not behind the wheel, teens with ADHD are more impulsive and get distracted more easily. The sensation-seeking component of ADHD may make them more likely than other teens to speed, to engage in driving games (such as races), and to drink and drive. These factors can spell real trouble. Teenagers with ADHD are about four times more likely to speed and to have accidents than other teenage drivers.

Some experts recommend that young people with ADHD wait a little longer to start driving. (Insurance companies, law enforcement agencies, and hospitals undoubtedly support this suggestion, too!) There is a real, biological reasoning to this plan. In your late teens, your body chemistry changes enough that your ADHD symptoms (especially those associated with hyperactivity and impulsiveness) are likely to decline. A little more life experience in general can also make a major difference in your ability to make good judgments. When you do begin to drive, keep one rule in mind: A car is a tool, not a toy. Use it safely!

Dating

Dating brings up a whole different set of issues. It can be extremely hard to share that you have ADHD with a person you want to impress. How much you tell them should probably depend on the kind of relationship you expect to have. Among all the advice you'll get, remember that a person who really cares about you will want to know about all the things that impact your life, good and bad. Sharing that you have ADHD might actually improve your relationship by helping that person understand how you respond and why.

You'll also have to watch out for being too impulsive when it comes to sex. Attraction makes everyone giddy, and even people who aren't impulsive find it extremely difficult to know where to draw the line. Paying attention as you go along will help a lot. Give some thought to what's happened so far and what might come up next. Consider your responses in advance. And best of all, talk with the other person. He or she may feel just as nervous (or as reckless) as you do. You might even want to ask a trusted adult for some advice.

Many families find that it's useful to discuss the dating issue in advance, so that rules and expectations are clear. Your parents may want to meet the person before you go out or may limit your activities to certain settings. (For example, you might be allowed to go out to a restaurant or an arcade but are restricted from places where no adults are present.) Parents may even decide that you shouldn't date until you reach a certain age. It can be helpful for you to write

[The Chemistry of Love]

At some point in your teenage years or young adulthood, you are almost certain to fall in love. When you do, an amazing thing might happen: your ADHD symptoms could actually begin to let up a bit. That's because love causes real, measurable chemical changes in our bodies. One of these is an increase in levels of dopamine in the brain.

Love, and all the chemistry that goes with it, feels great—but it can also make you careless about things like taking your medication and keeping up your therapy. Even if ADHD symptoms ease when you are happy, it's important to remember that there is no actual cure for ADHD—not even love. And since love has its ups and downs, it's probably best to maintain your usual treatment regimen to help you through the difficult moments.

these expectations down together. They can then be posted, like other lists and schedules, around the house as a reminder—and you'll be more likely to remember to have them reconsidered now and then, too.

Family Relationships

Remember that ADHD is frequently passed from parents to children through genes. In other words, if you have ADHD, then chances are that one of your parents or a close relative also has it (though it may not have been diagnosed if that person is an adult). This isn't an excuse to go blaming your parents or diagnosing other family members, but it is a reminder that you are not alone.

Parents are often amazing supporters of their kids with ADHD. They may work tirelessly to find ways to make a child's life better and to improve the symptoms. This can take a great toll on their energy, however, and can sometimes even create problems between parents. No matter how much they may care about each other and share the goal of helping their kids, parents sometimes disagree on how to deal with a child's ADHD. And even if they understand that ADHD is a genetic disorder that is beyond their control, parents can experience a deep sense of guilt. This can add to the family's stress and make it hard to agree on treatment plans. In the case of parents who have other marital problems, dealing with the complexities of ADHD can become overwhelming. If you are in this kind of situation, it's important to remember that it's not your fault.

Marriages (and all relationships) are complex and require constant work to maintain. Under the best or worst of circumstances, families often benefit from therapy to resolve problems.

Brothers and sisters also contribute to the family's dynamic. They may be supportive, or you may fight nonstop. Some of the frustrations they experience are legitimate. Your needs may seem to overshadow theirs, and you may seem to get more attention for your everyday successes than they do. Likewise, you might feel irritated by your siblings' lack of understanding or by their apparent "perfection." This is where you can play an important role. Do your best to avoid taking your frustrations out on them, bullying them, or demanding extra attention because of your ADHD. One positive action is to educate

your siblings (and anyone else who will listen) about the challenges and benefits of your particular type of ADHD. Likewise, try to learn about their challenges and skills—we all have them—and then be supportive.

It's tough to be part of a family. Even when you are related by blood to your family members, it's amazing how different each individual is. And that can lead to conflict. The only real solution is communication. Of course, it's not always easy to communicate with other people—even those you are related to. They see the world differently than you, and they have different priorities, fears, and goals. But the alternative—growing up in a home where everyone is unhappy—is not an option.

Talking allows you to air your feelings, and it's a way to set up guidelines for behavior—yours and others'—that make your home a more livable place. Even though they care about you, your family members will still sometimes get frustrated when you forget your homework, bail on a family outing, or miss an important appointment. They'll do things that drive you up the wall, too. The solution? Be honest. Be open—and open-minded. Take responsibility for the things that are your own: your health, your attitude, your schoolwork and learning, your relationships. Ask for reasonable rules—and then follow them.

Believe it or not, most of those irritating rules your parents set up are not arbitrary—and they can actually make your life a lot easier. Curfews help you stay on task and keep track of time. The need to speak nicely to others forces you to slow down and

Getting an outside point
of view can be helpful.
Arrange some family
counseling sessions to resolve
long-term problems or to
handle issues when
they come up. Remember,
too, that people around
you have separate lives and
often have problems of their
own. Caring about their
issues and listening to
your family members can go
a long way toward improving
communication—and
it's likely to make them a
little bit more patient
at times when you
need to be the focus
of attention.

consider your words or to take a break when you are upset. Apologizing (or at least acknowledging the feelings of others in response to your actions) can also be remarkably satisfying. Even the process of making mistakes can have benefits. By examining the situation in your mind afterward, you can see what went wrong and where—and then you can make a plan for how to avoid that situation (and similar ones) later.

One important life skill for you will be to pay close, honest attention to your actions. Learn to recognize (even if it's in hindsight) when your ADHD kicks in and causes a problem for you or others. In time, if you really try, you can begin recognizing signs as they happen or immediately afterward. Then you can avoid these triggers, making your life and others' much easier. And let's be honest: sometimes it's easy to use your symptoms to get out of taking responsibility—for example, when you choose to play on the computer all evening rather than doing your homework and then blame your ADHD for making you lose track of time. Everyone has trouble "keeping it together" at times, but don't let your ADHD be a crutch to explain away the times when you know you can do better. Instead, take control of your actions and take pride in the successes that will result.

[Tidy Room, Tidy Mind]

One of the biggest daily challenges for people with ADHD is organization. Your parents may already nag you about having a messy room, so this is a great place to start getting organized—not just because they expect it of you, but because it will really improve your life. Then see where your "mess" flows out into the rest of the house and begin to make some improvements. (It's a radical idea, but you might even go so far as to tidy up your part of the car or your locker at school.)

- Decide on particular places to keep important items, such as your keys, money, and schoolbooks.
- Try color-coding the drawers in your furniture, with one color for each type of clothing, school or art supply, etc. (Baskets in your closet or on bookshelves can serve a similar purpose.) Then make a habit of putting items back in the correct place after every use, rather than leaving them randomly around the room.
- Set up a daily routine to help you get things done. For example, put your laundry in the hamper as soon as you take off your clothes, and feed your pet first thing after school. Take the trash out right after dinner each night.
- If a routine is still too random for you, write up schedules and lists of chores, homework, and other tasks. This will give you concrete goals to meet. Place copies around the house in obvious places such as the door of the refrigerator or a bulletin board in your room. That way you'll be reminded often of what needs to be done. What a sense of accomplishment when you can check things off—and what a relief not to be nagged!

chapter 7

The Future Can Be Bright

Attention-deficit/hyperactivity disorder looks daunting when you just focus on the symptoms and diagnosis. While it would be naïve to deny that ADHD creates challenges for people who have it, it also imparts some wonderful benefits. People with ADHD are often full of humor, charm, and playfulness. They are creative and spontaneous. They speak their minds, are insightful, and show a strong sense of commitment to the things and people they love. Energy and enthusiasm are very often part of the ADHD package as well, providing the fuel to get difficult things done. Even the tendency toward risk taking,

"Being ADD, when I
read a book about marine
life my mind allows me
to travel with the fish
and imagine life beneath
the sea. Or I can read
a book about astronomy
and dance among
the stars.... I may not
immediately comprehend
that 3+4=7, but I may
fully realize that n+26=51
and that the missing
number is 25."

—Matthew Kutz, age 13[1]

when done consciously, can be a powerful skill. Many people enjoy the fact that their ADHD helps them see the world in unique ways—and they learn to use the symptoms to their own advantage. In fact, some experts believe that many of history's greatest achievers actually had (or have) ADHD.

Told by teachers he would never be able to learn well or succeed in life, Thomas Edison was taken out of school at the age of seven and taught at home by his mother. Success came for Edison in his twenties, but throughout his life he had a habit of flitting from one project to another. Fortunately for us, he eventually finished most of them, and by the end of his life in 1931, he had patented at least a thousand inventions. Among these are the modern lightbulb, the record player (predecessor to CD players), and alkaline

"I prefer to distinguish ADD as attention abundance disorder. Everything is just so interesting ... remarkably at the same time."

—Frank Coppola[2]

batteries (the common batteries used in flashlights and many other consumer products).

Albert Einstein's parents worried because it took him a long time to learn to speak as a child. He was very awkward in social situations and frequently got into trouble for cutting school or failing to pay attention. He went on to discover the relationship between energy and matter (which is expressed in the famous equation $E=mc^2$) and to describe how the speed at which an object moves affects time. In 1921, he was awarded the Nobel Prize in Physics.

Einstein displayed many symptoms of ADHD and got poor grades in school. Today he is remembered as one of the most accomplished and creative scientists of all time.

After examining these men's life stories, experts have suggested that both probably had ADHD. Yet both accomplished great things, despite early signs of being different, slow, or difficult.

While not everyone can be an Einstein, anyone with ADHD can do truly world-altering things—both in spite of their ADHD and because of it. Two outstanding examples are Michael Phelps and Danielle Fisher. Phelps won six gold medals and two bronze medals at the 2004 Summer Olympics in Athens, Greece, breaking three Olympic swimming records along the way. Fisher is a mountain climber who, in 2005 at the age of twenty, became the youngest person to successfully climb the highest mountain peak on each continent. Both athletes were diagnosed with ADHD as children. They believe that ADHD gave them the drive and energy to reach their goals.[3,4]

The words of the great scientist Isaac Newton can serve as a good reminder of the beauty of being different. "I do not know what I may appear to the world," he wrote, "but to myself I seem to have been only like a boy playing on the sea shore and diverting himself and then finding a smoother pebble or a prettier shell than ordinary, whilst the greater ocean of truth lay all undiscovered before me."

"More and more, the concept of ADD as a disorder is being qualified by inclusion of a string of positive qualities— such as creativity, high intelligence, ability to do many things at once, an aptitude for small business entrepreneurship, and a powerful intuitive sense."

—Susan Burgess[5]

The challenges of ADHD don't have to prevent you from doing great things and living a full life. Just look at Cynthia Gerdes, for example. Gerdes is one of the owners of Creative Kidstuff, an award-winning chain of toy stores that began in Minnesota's Minneapolis–St. Paul area. In the early 1980s, Gerdes was working on her master's degree in business at the University of Minnesota. As part of a class assignment, she wrote a business plan that proposed a unique kind of toy store. She was so excited by the idea that she quit school to pursue making the store a reality. Today, two decades after the first store opened, Creative Kidstuff has six stores in the Minneapolis area, as well as branches in many airports and displays in several major department stores.[6]

The success of Creative Kidstuff isn't random, and it didn't happen because of luck. Inspired and energized by her idea, Gerdes took a huge risk by borrowing some of her parents' retirement savings to start her first store. She worked long hours every day to get it going and to manage all the complicated business details. All along the way, she stuck to her own commitment that learning and fun should go hand in hand.

You won't find cheap or violent toys at Creative Kidstuff. Instead, the shelves (and the floor and the ceiling) are filled with books, music, instruments, art supplies, puzzles, science games, and other toys that spark a kid's imagination. Kids walk in and squeal with delight; parents enter and sigh with relief at such an unusual, inspiring collection of toys. Believing that toy guns make children insensitive to violence, Gerdes has even sponsored several campaigns encouraging kids to bring their toy guns to Creative Kidstuff stores for disposal. The success of those campaigns, which have collected thousands of guns, shows that many kids get the point: play should be healthy and imaginative, not hurtful or driven by the storylines of television shows.

Gerdes credits ADHD for her innovative ideas, boundless energy, and willingness to take such big risks. She also knows that ADHD makes her easily distracted, and she admits it's hard to sit still through all the long meetings that are part of running a successful business. The flip side to those habits, which others might see as frustrating, is that she is able to juggle many tasks at once—and always with a focus on the fun.

Long ago, Gerdes opted not to use medication to treat her ADHD, knowing that she'd rather deal with the complexities of her symptoms than suppress them and risk losing her "edge." Her choice is not for everyone—Gerdes recognizes that her ADHD is mild enough to be handled with behavioral modifications. Other people might not have the same experience.[7] Still, her story proves that having ADHD—or being different in any way—can be an enriching part of life. And who knows? It may even lead you to greatness.

[glossary]

amphetamines—a group of drugs that stimulates production of certain neurotransmitters in the nervous system

assessment—a process used to determine whether a person has ADHD, including input from medical professionals, parents, and teachers

chromosomes—long strands of protein found in the nucleus of every cell, which carry genetic information inherited from parents

comorbidities—disorders that accompany other medical conditions

disorder—a medical condition that affects how the body or mind functions

dopamine—a chemical produced by nerve cells that helps control fine-motor movements and inhibits impulsive behaviors; it is a neurotransmitter that can affect ADHD symptoms

genes—specific regions on chromosomes that control particular parts of the body's growth, development, and functioning

genetics—the study of heredity and how physically inherited traits are passed from parent to child

hyperactivity—extremely active or restless behavior

impulses—electrical signals that flow along a nerve cell; also used to describe actions that are taken without thinking

impulsivity—a tendency to act or speak without thinking

inattention—an inability to focus attention on one activity for a sustained period of time

metabolism—the body's process of building or breaking down chemicals to fuel the body's functions and sustain life

neurons—cells in the nervous system that carry impulses to cause reactions

neurotransmitters—chemical "messengers" that help carry impulses through the nervous system

norepinephrine—also called noradrenaline, it's a chemical produced by nerve cells that regulates emotions and attentiveness; it is a neurotransmitter that can affect ADHD symptoms

rebound—the experience when medications wear off and symptoms return at a higher level

receptors—"docking stations" on the surface of a nerve cell, to which neurotransmitters attach

remission—a lessening or disappearance of symptoms of a medical condition

sensation-seeking behavior—the pursuit of new, stimulating experiences; often involves risk taking

serotonin—a chemical produced by nerve cells that affects moods, sleep, awareness of pain, body temperature, and appetite; it is a neurotransmitter that can affect ADHD symptoms

stimulant—a type of drug that increases the nervous system's production of dopamine or other neurotransmitters

stimuli—plural of *stimulus*; occurrences in the surrounding environment that catch a person's attention

synapse—a point at which a nerve impulse passes from one neuron to the next

tics—habitual movements of the body that are beyond a person's conscious control

[to find out more]

Books

Beal, Eileen. *Everything You Need to Know about ADD/ADHD*. The Need to Know Library. New York: The Rosen Publishing Group, 1998.

Beal, Eileen. *Ritalin: Its Use and Abuse*. The Drug Abuse Prevention Library. New York: The Rosen Publishing Group, 1999.

Covey, Sean. *The 7 Habits of Highly Effective Teens*. New York: Fireside, 1998.

Heron, Ronald W., and Val J. Peter. *A Good Friend: How to Make One, How to Be One*. Boys Town, Neb.: Boys Town Press, 1998.

Levine, Mel. *Keeping a Head in School: A Student's Book about Learning Disabilities and Learning Disorders*. Cambridge, Mass.: Educators Publishing Service, 1990. (Also available in audiotape form)

Nadeau, Kathleen. *Help 4 ADD@HighSchool.*
Altamonte Springs, Fla.: Advantage Books, 1998.

Parker, Steve. *The Brain and Nervous System.* Our
Bodies. Chicago: Raintree, 2004.

Quinn, Patricia O., ed. *ADD and the College Student:
A Guide for High School and College Students with
Attention Deficit Disorder.* Washington, D.C.:
Magination Press, 1994.

Quinn, Patricia O., and Judith M. Stern. *Putting on
the Brakes: Young People's Guide to Understanding
Attention Deficit Hyperactivity Disorder.* Washington,
D.C.: Magination Press, 2001.

Walker, Beth. *The Girls' Guide to ADHD: Don't Lose
This Book!* Bethesda, Md.: Woodbine House, 2004.

Walker, Pam. *The Brain and Nervous System.*
Understanding the Human Body. Farmington Hills,
Mich.: Lucent Books, 2003.

Magazines and Newsletters

ADDvance Magazine
http://www.addvance.com/

Children's Additude Magazine
http://www.additudemag.com/ourkids.asp

Multimedia Resources

Bramer, Jennifer, and Wilma Fellman. *Success in College and Career with Attention Deficit Disorder*. Plantation, Fla.: Specialty Press, 1997.

Generation *RX: Reading, Writing, and Ritalin*. New York: A&E Home Video, 2001.

Gordon, Michael. *Jumpin' Johnny Get Back to Work!* DeWitt, N.Y.: GSI Publications, 1994. (Book and video/DVD set)

Rief, Sandra. *How to Help Your Child Succeed in School: Strategies and Guidance for Parents of Children with ADHD and/or Learning Disabilities*. San Diego: Educational Resource Specialists, 1997.

Online Sites

ADHD Gets Some Attention
(from the University of Washington)
http://faculty.washington.edu/chudler/adhd.html

ADHD.com
(from Eli Lilly and Company)
http://www.adhd.com/index.jsp

The ADHD e-Book
(from the Pediatric Neurology Associates)
http://www.pediatricneurology.com/adhd.htm

How Your Brain Works
(from HowStuffWorks)
http://health.howstuffworks.com/brain8.htm
Don't miss the video on page 2 of this site!

Multiple Intelligences and ADHD
(from the Salem, New Hampshire, School District)
http://www.atc.unh.edu/~fisk/MIIntro.html

Nervous System Guide: Tour Your Neural Circuits
(from the National Science Teachers Association)
http://www.nsta.org/nerves/

Neuroscience for Kids
(from the University of Washington)
http://faculty.washington.edu/chudler/neurok.html

Teens' Health: ADD and ADHD
(from the Nemours Foundation)
http://kidshealth.org/teen/school_jobs/school/adhd.html

Organizations

Attention Deficit Disorder Association (ADDA)
P.O. Box 543
Pottstown, PA 19464
(484) 945-2101
http://www.add.org/

Children and Adults with Attention-Deficit/Hyperactivity Disorder (CHADD)
8181 Professional Place, Suite 150
Landover, MD 20785
(800) 233-4050
http://www.chadd.org/

Learning Disabilities Association of America
4156 Library Road
Pittsburgh, PA 15234
(412) 341-1515
http://www.ldanatl.org/

[source notes]

CHAPTER ONE

1. PsychNet-UK, "DSM-IV Disorder Information Sheet: Attention-Deficit/Hyperactivity Disorder (Hyperkinetic Disorders)," http://www.psychnet-uk.com/dsm_iv/attention_deficit_disorder.htm.
2. The Children's Clinic, "Attention-Deficit/Hyperactivity Disorder, ADHD," http://www.thechildrensclinic.ie/adhd.html.
3. Edward M. Hallowell and John J. Ratey, "The Evolution of a Disorder," http://www.pbs.org/wgbh/pages/frontline/shows/medicating/adhd/evolution.html.
4. National Institute of Mental Health, *Attention Deficit Hyperactivity Disorder* (Bethesda, Md.: National Institutes of Health, 2003), NIMH Publication #3572.
5. National Mental Health Association, "Children's Mental Health Statistics," http://www.nmha.org/children/prevent/stats.cfm.

6. National Institute on Drug Abuse, "NIDA InfoFacts: Methylphenidate (Ritalin)," http://www.nida.nih.gov/Infofacts/Ritalin.html.

7. PBS Frontline, "Medicating Kids: What Happens to ADHD Kids?" http://www.pbs.org/wgbh/pages/frontline/shows/medicating/adhd/study.html.

8. National Institutes of Health, "Severe Childhood ADHD May Predict Alcohol, Substance Abuse Problems in Teen Years," http://www.nih.gov/news/pr/aug2003/niaaa-17.htm.

CHAPTER TWO

1. National Institute of Mental Health, *Attention Deficit Hyperactivity Disorder* (Washington, D.C.: U.S. Department of Health and Human Services, 2003).

2. AllCare Behavioral Services, "Psychological Testing: Quick Reference," http://allcare.net/s2/testingResources.php.

3. Jeffrey N. Epstein et al, "Relations between Continuous Performance Test Performance Measures and ADHD Behaviors—Attention Deficit Hyperactivity Disorder," *Journal of Abnormal Child Psychology*, October 2003.

4. Arthur L. Robin, *ADHD in Adolescents: Diagnosis and Treatment* (New York: The Guilford Press, 1998).

5. Ibid.

6. U.S. Environmental Protection Agency, "America's Children and the Environment (ACE)," http://www.epa.gov/envirohealth/children/emerging_issues/adhd.htm.

7. Robin, 1998.
8. Agency for Healthcare Research and Quality, "Diagnosis of Attention-Deficit/Hyperactivity Disorder," http://www.ahrq.gov/clinic/epcsums/adhdsutr.htm.
9. National Institute of Mental Health, *Attention Deficit Hyperactivity Disorder*.
10. Ibid.
11. Mohammed Bagheri et al, "Recognition and Management of Tourette's Syndrome and Tic Disorders," *American Family Physician* 59, no. 8 (April 15, 1999).
12. Agency for Healthcare Research and Quality.

CHAPTER THREE

1. How Stuff Works, "How Your Brain Works," http://health.howstuffworks.com/brain8.htm.
2. Medical News Today, "New Findings in ADHD," http://www.medicalnewstoday.com/medicalnews.php?newsid=4940.
3. McLean Hospital Developmental Biopsychiatry Research Program, "Development of Objective Tests to Aid in Diagnosis," http://www.mclean.harvard.edu/research/clinicalunit/dbrp/dotad.php.
4. McLean Hospital, "Researchers Locate Key Area of the Brain Impacted by ADHD," http://www.mclean.harvard.edu/news/press/archived/20000328_adhdnews.php.
5. BBC News, "Attention Drugs Do Not Shrink Brain," http://news.bbc.co.uk/1/hi/health/2307187.stm.

6. University of Washington, "Neuroscience for Kids: Neurotransmitters," http://staff.washington.edu/chudler/chnt1.html.

7. National Institute of Mental Health, *Attention Deficit Hyperactivity Disorder* (Washington, D.C.).

8. National Mental Health Association, "Children's Mental Health Statistics," http://nmha.org/children/prevent/stats.cfm.

9. Center for Children's Health and the Environment, "Attention Deficit/Hyperactivity Disorder (ADHD) and Environmental Exposures," http://www.childenvironment.org/factsheets/adhd.htm

10. Environmental Protection Agency, "Addressing Lead at Superfund Sites: Human Health," http://www.epa.gov/superfund/programs/lead/health.htm.

11. Center for Children's Health and the Environment, "Attention Deficit/Hyperactivity Disorder (ADHD) and Environmental Exposures."

12. Science Daily, "Very Low Birthweight Children Have Long-Term Behavioral and Psychiatric Consequences," http://www.sciencedaily.com/releases/1997/06/970606122249.htm.

CHAPTER FOUR

1. Edward M. Hallowell and John J. Ratey, "The Evolution of a Disorder," http://www.pbs.org/wgbh/pages/frontline/shows/medicating/adhd/evolution.html.

2. Children and Adults with Attention-Deficit/Hyperactivity Disorder, "CHADD Fact Sheet #3: Evidence-Based Medication Management for

Children and Adolescents with AD/HD," http://
www.chadd.org/fs/fs3.htm.

3. A.D.D. Coaching Group, "ADD Quotes," http://
www.addcoachinggroup.com/02_quotes.html.

4. American Academy of Pediatrics, "Clinical Practice
Guideline: Treatment of the School-Aged Child
with Attention-Deficit Hyperactivity Disorder,"
Pediatrics (October 21, 2001): pp. 1,033–1,044.

5. National Institute of Mental Health, *Attention
Deficit Hyperactivity Disorder* (Washington, D.C.).

6. Willow Lawson, "ADHD's Outdoor Cure,"
Psychology Today (March/April 2004).

7. Jane St. Clair, "Attention Deficit Hyperactivity
Disorder and 'Green Time,'"
http://www.4-adhd.com/greentimeadhd.html.

8. Richard Louv, *Last Child in the Woods: Saving Our
Children from Nature-Deficit Disorder* (Chapel Hill,
N.C.: Algonquin Books of Chapel Hill, 2005).

CHAPTER FIVE

1. National Institute of Mental Health, *Attention
Deficit Hyperactivity Disorder* (Washington, D.C.).

2. LDOnLine, "ADHD: Building Academic Success,"
http://www.ldonline.org/ld_indepth/add_adhd/
ael_success.html.

3. National Dissemination Center for Children with
Disabilities, "IDEA Law," http://www.nichcy.org/
idealaw.htm.

4. LDOnLine, "An Overview of ADA, IDEA, and
Section 504: Update 2001," http://www.ldonline.org/
ld_indepth/legal_legislative/update_504_2001.html.

5. A.D.D. Coaching Group,"ADD Quotes,"http://www. addcoachinggroup.com/02_quotes.html.

6. Grad L. Flick, *How to Reach and Teach Teenagers with ADHD: A Step-by-Step Guide to Overcoming Difficult Behaviors at School and at Home* (West Nyack, N.Y.: The Center for Applied Research in Education, 2000).

CHAPTER SIX

1. National Institute of Mental Health, *Attention Deficit Hyperactivity Disorder* (Washington, D.C.).

2. U.S. Environmental Protection Agency,"America's Children and the Environment (ACE),"http://www. epa.gov/envirohealth/children/emerging_issues/ adhd.htm.

3. Alan Logan,"New Findings about Omega-3 Fatty Acids and Depression,"http://www.mercola. com/2004/feb/14/omega_3_depression.htm.

4. Eugene Arnold et al,"Serum Zinc Correlates with Parent- and Teacher-Rated Inattention in Children with Attention-Deficit Hyperactivity Disorder," http://psychmed.osu.edu/articles/zinc_in_ADHD. cap.2005.15.628.pdf.

5. Jim Dryden,"Kids with ADHD May Smoke to Treat Their Inattention Problems,"http://news-info. wustl.edu/tips/page/normal/200.html.

6. National Sleep Foundation,"Teens & Sleep," http://www.sleepfoundation.org/hottopics/index. php?secid=18&id=264.

CHAPTER SEVEN

1. Born to Explore! The Other Side of ADD, "Positive Quotes about ADD," http://borntoexplore. org/addquo~1.htm.
2. A.D.D. Coaching Group, "ADD Quotes," http://www.addcoachinggroup.com/02_quotes.html.
3. Life with ADHD, "Danielle Fisher Sets Mountain Climbing Record," HYPERLINK "http://www.lifewithadhd.com/archives/famous_people_with_addadhd/danielle_fisher_sets_mountain_climbing_record.php" http://www.lifewithadhd.com/archives/famous_people_with_addadhd/danielle_fisher_sets_mountain_climbing_record.php.
4. Paul McMullen, "A Reluctant Prodigy: Michael Phelps Had to Be Dragged onto the Road to Swimming Greatness," *Baltimore Sun*, August 8, 2004.
5. Born to Explore! The Other Side of ADD, "Positive Quotes about ADD."
6. Peg Meier, "The Secret of Her Success?" *Minneapolis Star-Tribune*, May 11, 2005.
7. Cynthia Gerdes, personal communication, July 2005.

[index]

[about the author]

Christine Petersen is a middle school science teacher who lives near Minneapolis, Minnesota. When she is not writing or teaching, Christine spends time with her young son and enjoys snowshoeing, canoeing, and bird watching. She is a member of the Society of Children's Book Writers and Illustrators and is the author of more than a dozen books for Children's Press and Franklin Watts.